Amazon FBA

A Scientific Breakdown of How to Build Your Own Profitable Amazon FBA Business

Table of Contents

Introduction 1

Chapter 1 What is Amazon F.B.A.? 2

Chapter 2 How to Get Started 3

Chapter 3 Using platforms to sell products through Amazon FBA 8

Chapter 4 Where to source the best inventory 18

Chapter 5 Amazon FBA Private Label Sourcing 23

Chapter 6 How to make money 31

Chapter 7 Increasing Sales with Marketing 33

Chapter 8 Questions and Concerns 43

Conclusion 47

Introduction

I want to thank you and congratulate you for purchasing the book Amazon FBA: A Scientific Breakdown of How to Build Your Own Profitable Amazon FBA Business

This book will introduce you to the basics of Amazon FBA (or Fulfillment by Amazon).

The book will also provide you with step by step instructions on how to build a complete, profitable Amazon FBA business. You will also get tips on topics such as sourcing goods, marketing goods, and knowing how to avoid common pitfalls and challenges.

This book contains proven steps and strategies on how to become a truly savvy Amazon salesperson. The concepts behind Amazon FBA are simple. If you follow the information and tips in this book, you will have an advantage over the masses who will just set up a storefront and sell blindly.

Here's an inescapable fact: We want to make a profit when we start a business. You will miss opportunities and waste your resources unless you know how to make a profit *wisely*.

It's time for you to become an amazing business person who is proficient in the world of Amazon FBA!

Chapter 1
What is Amazon F.B.A.?

Amazon F.B.A. is both a concept and an activity. The acronym F.B.A. means "fulfilled by Amazon." In short, this way of doing business is setting your online store up in a way that the business behind Amazon.com is fulfilling your orders for your customers. For all intents and purposes, it appears that your product comes from Amazon, which is a dependable, world famous retailer.

When you sell through Amazon, or better put, if your customer's orders are fulfilled by Amazon, you will benefit from their professional services, their online platforms, and Amazon's reputation. Through Amazon FBA you may also use the virtual platforms of other sites such as eBay or Etsy, and still have Amazon "fulfill your order."

There are advantages to selling through Amazon, and this book will detail many of them. You will also learn of strategies for setting up your own online store, sourcing and marketing your products, selling them, and shipping them.

When you think of online commerce, you may think of purchasing goods by a brand name or by wide open options from different sources.

Chapter 2
How to Get Started

When you first embark upon starting an Amazon FBA business, you will want to familiarize yourself with Amazon's procedures and policies. These can be found on Amazon.com. On their website, Amazon states that "Ninety-three percent of sellers increase sales after joining Amazon FBA." We will discuss some of these in the chapters that follow.

When starting with Amazon FBA it is assumed that you will have a good, solid business plan. A good plan helps you to decide how to best buy and sell your items for a set and pre-planned profit. A good plan takes into account many things, including but not limited to expenses, into consideration.

After you have a business plan, you will also need to decide if you will resell items that you locate, find or make, or if you will create your own brand, which is referred to as "Amazon Private Label." There are some aspects to selling on Amazon, which are common to all types of selling/reselling, yet they are quite different in how they work.

Here is a quick list of the main types of e-commerce that you could delve into through Amazon.

Retail Arbitrage: Is when items are located and purchased online or they are purchased in local stores (small shops, antique stores, or larger retailers). They essentially are products made by others. This could be games, electronics, household items, etc. Retail arbitrage is also referred to "R.A." You would set up your virtual storefront using Amazon's platform.

Your own products: These can be products that you manufacture or craft. Perhaps you create bird houses or special jewelry that is one of a kind. You can post them for sale on an e-commerce site such as Amazon directly. You may have better luck posting them on other "platforms" as they are called, such as eBay and Etsy. Some people also use Craigslist. These platforms all can also be used with Retail arbitrage as well.

Part of this book will focus on how to find items, how to price them, how and where to resell them, and all of the other details of working with this type of e-commerce business.

Amazon Private Label: This way of using Amazon FBA involves purchasing bulk amounts of a product that you have sourced (usually from abroad), branding it with your own name, and then selling it through Amazon as your virtual storefront.

Depending on your goals, you may have some residual income, or you may find yourself with a full-time business at hand. It may be that you are looking for a business to build and expand. Each strategy above has different limitations, challenges, and types of successes. We will cover some of these throughout the book.

Each activity that you choose for your Amazon FBA business will take some thinking, and some calculations. Every expense that you have will offset your revenues, therefore each step should be a part of your smart business plan.

When you set up your business model, you will also want to decide if you want any investors, a partner, or live or virtual staff. Many people start their Amazon FBA with a home office.

If you chose to do it this way, you will have many benefits. You will need a central "hub" for your activity.

You won't need to rent space right away for your operations however if you start your business from home, you will have benefits that come with having a home office, that range from tax benefits and business expenses (including a business credit card that can actually help fuel your inventory). You should also locate a good accountant before you start your business who can walk you through these financial considerations. Use them as part of your business plan and to help you to proactively get organized.

With an of the e-commerce strategies through Amazon FBA, there is the same free market infrastructure. It is all about the supply and demand chain. You will at once be both buying and selling to make your profit. Any of the reselling or selling activities mentioned are created out of inefficiencies in the market. Consumers are looking for great and convenient deals. Sellers want a good profit. Where the two meet is where Amazon comes into play.

Here is a simple breakdown of how retail arbitrage works. While shopping intentionally or non-intentionally, you find products that seem to be at a discounted price. You can search websites to see what others are selling/buying for the same item. A retail arbitrage reseller would most likely buy 1 to 100 of the item and list them online if the cost and the potential sales price differential are worth the purchase.

You can also purchase an item from one site and sell on another. For example, you could buy something on Amazon then put the item or items for sale on eBay. Things that are generally unavailable sometimes make the item very desirable in this way.

Last but not least, is Fulfillment by Amazon or FBA. You could post an item on eBay, Etsy, or other sites and still have Amazon process it as if it was fulfilled by Amazon or FBA. This is a great way to tap into different markets with your product. We will later discuss how to select products and decide which markets are best however.

One concern that is valid but which has an appropriate response is the fear that there is too much competition. At first it may seem odd to sell something that so many other people have and also sell. In many cases, it is not just the rare and unavailable items that sell, but also commodities. However, you will learn that with reselling and selling, part of the lure to products is that they are desired, and when you make them unavailable at better rates, or rates with better shipping, they become more desirable. You will learn how to carve out your own market niche.

Much of what is sold with retail arbitrage is new with untouched packaging. There are categories within Amazon to designate whether an item is new or used, and in what condition however. If an item is new it is an easy decision for a comparison shopper, or an informed shopper at least, to know if the price is good. If it is a new item, and a brand name, consumers often will go with the lowest. They may already have trust in the brand, but they just need to see a vendor with better price or a better shipping offer to be convinced to make the purchase.

Some shoppers will pay whatever they need to or want to pay regardless of any factors. Some people will prefer to shop online versus a store, and won't mind paying a different price to avoid the trip. Low shipping prices may also play a part in that decision. PayPal and credit cards are very convenient ways for many online shoppers to buy things with convenience. Payment protections are also offered as an added layer of security for the customer, which makes online shopping more acceptable.

For a bunch of reasons, selling online works. Most consumers will purchase items once they locate exactly what they need. Some may purchase bundles that seem to be good value savings, or even just plain interesting. Many people do not shop and compare items. Other shoppers look at the differences between retail, Amazon, eBay, etc. Some shoppers have their usual sites or platforms where they prefer to shop. Interestingly, you will see that an item may be sold and coming through Amazon, but by way of retail arbitrage it may be sold on eBay for a bit more and it will still sell. As you can see, all shoppers have their needs and wants and there is room for all sellers.

Chapter 3
Using platforms to sell products through Amazon FBA

When you look at your business plan you will need to also research the workings of Amazon, eBay, Etsy, Craigslist, etc. As part of your business plan, you will build in strategies as to how to make a great profits with healthy margins. You will need to research and study each site, to include factors such as fees for the purchase processing, shipping, taxes and other fees for both the platform as well as Amazon. Once you set your dollar amount, you will design a profit margin formula to get there which will also include steps and strategies such as types of items, photos and item descriptions. All of these variables affect your prices.

Reselling and selling is a serious business. If you give it proper attention it will not just succeed but it can grow. As you will see with Private Label e-commerce, you also can scale up your business.

"Fulfillment by Amazon has a calculator to help you think about some of these variables. It is called "Fulfillment by Amazon Revenue" that can help to determine your profit. If you want to also compare your own product fulfillment costs and other orders that are "fulfilled by Amazon" or FBA, this calculator is helpful.

As mentioned earlier, reselling and selling is successful because price difference will always drive this online business model. It represents the future of buying and selling. Sources and marketplaces can be virtually anywhere, as are the consumers. E-Commerce is an increasingly huge part of the world economy.

As you get deeper into the Amazon FBA seller's world, there are complex business plans. For the purpose of this book we will keep it simple and streamlined, for the adventurous or for those who just desire to train with someone who has blazed the path already, you can find a coach or mentor who has been there and who has participated in Amazon FBA. It is a bit of a unique business strategy!

To sell items you will begin by establishing an account. Sites differ in many ways, including how they allow you to begin to list items and also how to sell the items as well. Sites like eBay have limits what you can list, or update, but on Amazon it could be as many as you like. You would use this information also to figure out your profit margin.

There are also some tips to using the various platforms that will help make it more efficient.

JoeLister, an automation tool, is one instrument that can help with sales, listing across sites and automatic updates providing access to more inventory and options. As you receive automated information updates, you can use that to readjust your price points and adjust what you need to adjust for the best profit margin as often as needed. This is a great tool especially if you have a lot of inventory.

Next we will provide a summary of how selling on Amazon through FBA would work. Think of FBA as having your own personal store where everything is virtually done for your, because you have outsourced all of the grunt work. You will still have work to do but it will be different. After you set up an account, you will go through a process of selecting what and how much of something to sell, and for how much. You (or your vendor) may ship your inventory to Amazon, where it is stored. Amazon will have workers pick your orders, pack them and ship the items for you.

Amazon directly tells you that you only need to:

- List
- Sell
- Ship
- Get paid

Of course there is more. This book will guide you through the important steps to work with Amazon FBA, aside from the obvious: listing key words and descriptions, and photos.

You will need to make sure that you read every single FBA page on Amazon's website. They have very clear and copious policies, and if you violate any of them, they could restrict your sales or close your store down entirely. You should also read up on their general mailing and shipping regulations.

Amazon will instruct you on various ways to use their services for your new e-commerce business. There are also different levels of services. Individual sellers or a Professional sellers on Amazon have different access, eligibilities and protocols. Your fees will also differ for transaction and sales, as well as picking, packing, shipping.

You can add inventory quite easily through Amazon FBA. Adding products can be done by manual additions, using buttons on the "store" pages, using software to add multiple items, uploading them on Amazon.

You can use the FBA system as well to get your stock to their warehouses. An Amazon "storage nexus" will hold your inventory. This is the place also where your orders are picked, packed, and then shipped. You also will be able to choose a carrier for your items. When you are at the point of setting costs and figuring out your margins, knowing the fees associated with all of these activities is very important.

Amazon has software that allows you to be alerted when you are low in stock on items. When stock dips to levels you have pre-set, you will automatically be told to order new inventory. If your stock is damaged or if it is missing, Amazon also will assist you. You could not have these guarantees even with just one neglectful employee in a local storefront!

Amazon's processes are smooth and they work. It is so much easier than if you had your own stock room to manage. Amazon will also arrange special storing positions and climate control your necessary items.

You can send smaller items to be picked and shipped or you could sent bulk amounts of items on pallets to an Amazon nexus. The Amazon FBA website will walk you through how to do this.

Amazon does charge storage fees for your inventory. There are also fees after items arrive, before they are sent to short-term or long term-storage or for removing inventory or disposing of your inventory. You can also set up an automatic removals by Amazon. This may be necessary for some items benefit if they have time limits, expiration dates, etc. For some sellers, they will opt to remove stock as well if needed to avoid the extra storage fees that are incurred with longer-term storage.

Fulfilled by Amazon (FBA) is about making a profit so everything that you do will center on having a good business strategy. You will need to think less like a shopper and more as a retailer however, which requires a new mindset.

Multi-channel fulfillment is a great complement to Amazon fulfillment. There are even tools through FBA that allow you to synchronize with your listings on eBay as well to keep them consistent. As you may know, the Amazon Marketplace includes both free and reduced shipping availability and so many other types of customer service offerings that would ripple over to customers using the other platforms, since it is FBA. With FBA, you have learned how Amazon will pick, pack, and ship your goods. This applies to goods that may be listed on eBay or Etsy. When you use multi-channel FBA, you always save money on storage, expenses, staffing, supplies, etc. and you can account for them all and control their expenses. Again, when you are establishing your products prices and setting profit margins this information is useful. Through Amazon FBA, even with the multi-channels, this is all spelled out for you from the beginning.

E-Bay

The site eBay.com is one of the primary Fulfillment by Amazon (FBA) Multi-Channel Fulfillment "platforms." Again, this allows you to work through Amazon to ship and sell and store goods on your behalf.

For now, this applies only to domestic inventory, but you do still have the option to ship things on your own as well, if needed. Listings on eBay have somewhat more limitations than if you were using Amazon directly. You should always read eBay's policies when setting up your account.

Selling from Amazon-to-eBay is interesting. A buyer most often does not care that an item came from Amazon necessarily. In most cases seeing an Amazon box is a good thing. However, many people also don't look at their packaging. We will cover this area later however.

Storage and shipping rates are usually quite good for the FBA Multi-channel Fulfillment. Low shipping costs can be set up as leverage for selling more than the competition on eBay. You do not get any Amazon commissions as you would if you are working directly through Amazon unfortunately however. This is one downside. Rates will be provided in easy tables however.

Price fluctuations between Amazon and eBay can affect your buying source materials, or even selling your items. Price fluctuations are unavailable though and it could affect your profits. This is something that may be difficult to keep up with but there are solutions for this problem that will be covered later.

Each multi-channel FBA requires different techniques and strategies.

Craigslist

Craigslist is usually a very easy way to buy and resell online. Local deals are a different target market. Most other sites are either domestic or international buyers.

When using Craigslist for sourcing goods, choose to view the listings with pictures. Also, you should try out different variations on words ordering and word stems (i.e., fence, fences, fencing, and wire fences). You can also try different state and regional listings. Adjacent states are also places where you can source new items.

Craigslist is intended to be used by locals. If you see something, most often you can go and see it before you buy it. That does not have to be the case, but that tends to be how it is arranged. If you want to purchase new or vintage items that you would like to see for yourself, this may be a good way to go. You potentially could set up shipping for products you sell yourself on the site however. Read the rules before you post.

When you first get on the site and do keyword searches, you can highlight what you see as your favorites using the star feature in Craigslist, and go back to them later. Compare similar items then go in for the buy if you are still interested. Yet act fast as thing son Craigslist do not usually last long, especially if they are of a really good quality and value.

Create a personal connection if you are looking to buy something especially if it is unique, large, or special in some way. Making a connection through a non-generic email sometimes will be a deciding factor. A seller may not want to part with a beloved or appreciated item that will go to just anyone. If you say you are interested do follow up and show up if you agree to meet. Craigslist has its own dynamics which differs from sites like eBay and Amazon.

Etsy

Many sellers and buyers also go to Etsy.com. Etsy provides specialty, hand crafted, one of a kind, or limited productions of many different items. Each Etsy seller has their own virtual store. A quick look on the site www.etsy.com will tell you a lot.

Take a look through at the type of products that sell on Etsy. You will gather much information on the markets, types of shoppers and sellers and the unique niches that it serves.

With Etsy (like other sites) pictures are important. Perhaps with Etsy, the pictures are even more relevant, given that most of what is there can be considered to be art in some form. You won't see what you may see often on sites like amazon where a generic photo is used for the same product across sellers.

The item descriptions are also important as are goo descriptions that pop. The descriptions should not be vague. The items on Etsy are generally not what you would find on a retail or department store site, therefore they need to have great selling points. Personalized descriptions also help draw buyers. You should differentiate your items from the rest in the best way that you possibly can.

Setting up for Selling

Photographs should be of high quality. Use original work. If you must use a generic, box photo, make sure you describe why (perhaps it is not out of the pristine box). But be sure that the box is not bent, ripped, or stained or you will have misled a buyer. You also do not want to have someone do the same to you if you are going to source your materials. Do not portray an item as it was in its original state if it is used, say so. Be descriptive.

Using generic photos may be passable in Amazon (with appropriate tagging and information as described prior). However, eBay and Etsy should require original photos and descriptions. Amazon will want to know specifically if something is categorized as Used, New, or Like New. Color, measurements, or other details as well.

Search Engine Optimization or S.E.O. will help you with priming your descriptions. You will want to learn as much as you can about this as you get into effectively marketing your items. Getting them to show up on a website that Google recognizes quickly is going to be key with any e-commerce. You must learn about Search Engine Optimization (SEO) if you want to be successful selling online with Amazon FBA. SEO helps to increase the customer exposure to your product information. You should know some basic Search Engine Optimization but you can also find someone who is much more and well versed. Someone who is good at SEO knows how to convert searches in to sales.

Make sure that you read and research not just Amazon's information but also any site that you plan to connect to your Amazon FBA business plan. Each platform or site also has ways to help you with your sales. Your sales are their sales, so they are invested in providing you with tools and features to inform and assist you. One such tool is "eBay Radio" which provides live and recorded podcasts that help resellers maximize their products. It is unique to eBay.

For more tips for other platforms, watch out for user forums. You also may see comments on a site forum or a newsletter that may be helpful to you. Some may also host podcasts or YouTube channels. Others have Facebook pages or groups.

Increasing Sales

If you would like to scale up your business you may want to consider Amazon Private Label as well. This book will provide more information in a later chapter.

There are some software programs out there that can also be tools for your Amazon FBA business. Let us look at the program called PriceYak. Amongst other features, the PriceYak program offers:

- Listings for products the original source site where your products are from.

- Automatic orders for items that are sold on your site.

- Management tools to track mailed orders.

- Repricing lists when prices change, but automatically.

This is much more cost effective than paying staff or using your own valuable time.

Price fluctuations in different platforms may complicate things for you through Amazon FBA. For example, an order placed through one site where pricing may have gone down on another may change your profit margin. It also affects your positioning against your competition. The software automates the processes and thinks this part through for you. Being able to quickly and efficiently track changes also helps you make better decisions.

Chapter 4
Where to source the best inventory

Always know your market for selling products and for sourcing them to sell. Certain platforms do better with certain items. You should study these differences as well. For example, Craigslist is excellent for furniture, materials, and technology, and eBay or Amazon is better for books and clothing.

Do some market research when you create your business plan and goals. This is a serious aspect to your business and it is not the same as merely shopping because you like something. You do not want to spend money on stockpiles of things that never leave the shelves.

If you have ever held a tag sale, or have donated goods and had to track their value, you have had to look at quality and cost. You can start small by selling something in your home. Apps such as Profit Bandit also allow you to find current market prices for items anywhere that you want to try to sell on Amazon FBA!

What now follows are descriptions of the most common areas for sourcing individual or bulk items.

Many warehouses want to get rid of old items and clean stock shelves. You may even find going out of business sales. Many warehouses will sell pallets full of items. You will find out about some by roadside signs, newspaper ads, Craigslist and other similar listing sites or other media.

Don't fear the amount of stock once you get deeper into your Amazon FBA business. That is what the Amazon nexus is for! You may not need it right away but you will at some point.

With liquidators, you will have access to supplies and overages due to bankruptcy, retirement, buy-outs or close-outs of other businesses. Liquidators are vying to get rid of their stock to pay off debts, creditors, vendors, etc. etc. You can often haggle and negotiate as well, since they are desperate and forced to do something quickly.

Many list serves, mailing lists, newspapers, online sites (like Craigslist), and digital newsletters tell where local and state governments often sell unclaimed or seized items at auctions Large government agencies (i.e., federal, some state) may sell unused, extra items, and used goods that they are able to sell at auctions that are open to the public as well. You can also pay for access to other sites.

Changes of seasons and major holidays create overages for many retail stores. Sales are abundant and this is when you will catch great deals. You will also catch great deals when older items are being cleared from shelves and overstock. Back-to-school also offers a "seasonal" sale period, as do big celebrations, and even sports and other public events that translate into merchandise. These are great ways to source inventory for your Amazon FBA.

Like any good shopper, you can ask for a deal if you were to purchase large amounts of items and supplies. Similar to warehouses, the store might even allow you to purchase a pallet-size bunch of an item. With some retailers you do want to be sure you have the proper reseller paperwork however. We will cover this later. States each have their own specific rules about this type of shopping, and specific stores can be finicky.

You should also use your Apps to do price comparisons. You can also always hop on websites such as eBay and Amazon when shopping to see what going rates are for the same or similar products.

Manufacturers sometimes sell items when they need to be turned over for fresh stock or new products. Take some time to locate a few good manufacturers and start to get to know them personally if possible.

Wholesalers also sometimes have clearance sales and may be another good resource. You have to do some research to find some that will be agreeable. Also it is advised to look at forums, blogs and Facebook groups to learn how others work with wholesalers and manufacturers. They also may be finicky about what they will do for you, and/or they may not be able to sell to a reseller at all.

As you move throughout your daily life you will find inspiration for seeing individual items or bulk products. You may also find yourself developing personal business contacts with people who can connect you somehow to some aspect of your amazon FBA, be it to sell, resell, buy, or market.

Retail stores can be a bit tricky as the quality will vary greatly from place to place. You can usually make purchases both person or online however which is convenient.

There are also creative ways to get inventory for your Amazon FBA stock. Many persons rack up copious amounts of discount cards, points, and rewards coupons which give more buying power for sourcing. There are also cash-back websites that you can sign up for. Coupon sites like retailmenow.com also help access discounts. Some mailing lists and list serves give you a heads up as to great deals and sales. Sometimes memberships allow access to great products as well. Gift cards are also popular. You also will see many gift card resellers on the web, including the multichannel platforms.

Platforms such as Amazon, eBay, Craigslist and Etsy are great places to source inventory to source through FBA. When developing your business plan, you should check out Amazon's "profit calculator" to determine pricing.

Some great websites such as Aliexpress, Alibaba, or Newegg are great for computer equipment, some clothing articles and other products. You may have a minimum or maximum quantity of goods that can be sold.

Consignment stores and thrifts shops are great places to locate unique or vintage items, souvenirs or memorabilia. Use your App to see what things might be worth, use a site like eBay to help as well. For some more important items you may want to take photographs and consult an expert in that area. You never know what you might find! Appliances, car parts, and machines may be bought to fix and sell through salvage yards as well.

"Picking" is the art of going to homes, barns, garages and storage areas including units, containers, and rooms that are unwanted and in some cases have been abandoned. The idea with picking is to either buy for yourself, or when doing FBA, to source inventory and buying at a lower market value and reselling higher.

You may be able to buy directly or you may have to participate in auctions Auctions are sometimes held for certain items, and other times they may be blind. With contents of storage units for example, it is common to auction off the container or room before anyone knows the value of the actual contents.

Attending estate sales is also a variation on tag sales and picking themes!

Chapter 5
Amazon FBA Private Label Sourcing

Sourcing for private label products to sell on Amazon FBA is a unique twist on Amazon FBA. You can choose to sell your own private label products through Amazon and also through other platform sites, as FBA. Choosing a private label product to sell, sourcing it, and getting it out there can be a challenge but the following pages will detail this popular form of e-commerce.

On occasion, there are people who sell on Amazon who may have successful item coupled with a bustling market. Some may have one but not the other, and they may still make a profit. When you don't have either of the two, you will find that your experience will be difficult and losing money may be imminent. The idea is to grow your profits, so planning as best as you can may help to prevent too great of losses.

We should also address that this is not *retail arbitrage* which means reselling someone else's product. This model of using a private label to sell on Amazon and other platforms through FBA relies on building a brand. To establish and sell a private label you will need to locate and source a product (most likely from Asia), that you can put your own brand on, import, and sell on Amazon under your new private label.

This type of business is also unlike *retail arbitrage* in that it is scalable and retail arbitrage is not so much so scalable. Retail arbitrage also focuses on short-term profit NOW. You want to build assets for long-term growth. Your asset is your brand. A brand is also part of a business that is capable of being sold if you would like to do so in the future.

Let us look at how to see what products are best for each type of market and platform for your FBA model.

Selecting a product or items

You probably want to find some type of product unless you have one concretely in mind. You will NEED to find something that will make you a profit as well. For this you will have to do proper research.

Amazon Private Label involves the following: locating cheap sources or suppliers, purchasing bulk of that product or item, putting your own brand on the product or item, sending it to a domestic Amazon nexus, marketing and listing the product, selling it and repeating steps in this process.

Buy at low costs. Items should be sellable around $5, $10, 15. You want quick and easy purchases. They will be in that range. The most you should sell at for this type of business model would be in the range of $50-$60 on the high end (with some exceptions, of course). Items that are cheaper to make, less expensive to ship, that withstand shipping wear, and have few (potentially breakable) pieces are recommended best practice.

If the customer has to spend a lot of time to research and read reviews or get opinions from others you may lose the sales with time delays. Private label products should ideally sell themselves easily.

Most private labels products come from Asia, namely, China where large amounts of products can be bought at lower costs. Research some websites to see charges for producing the same or very similar products before you buy.

Just as with the Tools discussed prior, there are tools for automating the pricing for your Private Label sourced goods.

Some programs will pull up items by like or related key words. You can determine sales and income estimates based on these automated programs.

Determining your buying costs will include many considerations. As a general rule of thumb, costs should be at about 1/4th of your selling price for the best profit margins.

You will want your sourced goods to be light weight. They will also be cheaper to ship because of their weight. To be worth your money to source, they have to be worthwhile also to ship. Strive for your items to weigh one to two pounds as a ballpark figure. Small and light items are easier. If it can fit in your hand or hands that would be ideal. If your items are larger the shipping and fees will increase and your profit margins will be lowered.

Amazon does tack on handling charges, packing and shipping costs to sellers at the time of sales. This should also figure into your profit margin calculations. Amazon's website pages for FBA and Private Label all contain areas where the shipping, handling, and other fees are listed. You will want to be familiar with these terms. When taking these fees into consideration now you know that you would need to buy the product for less than 20% of the sales price including the shipping charges just to be safe.

When you purchase items from your source/supplier you will know the dimensions and the item's weight before and with shipping as well. Product details for the same or similar products that you will need for calculations (and that you will want to have listed on Amazon or other platforms) are also found easily on other websites as well.

Find items that are mostly one piece, and that have one major purpose. Avoid items with breakable parts, tiny parts, convoluted instructions and so forth. You will frustrate buyers, you may have greater returns, customer dissatisfaction and it could lead to bad reviews which are critical.

Chose best sellers since you will see that there is an obvious market that you can fill, but with your own private label. Competitors see value in selling their product, and so should you.

Try to look for products with what is called a "best seller ranking" in Amazon of the 10,000-5,000 range (others may advise you to look around 500-200). It is odd to see such a difference, but various sellers have different experiences. You can also look to other sources such as eBay to see if your product or a similar product is in demand on multiple channels as well. Basically, the best seller ranking works because the higher the number of the ranking, the less a product sells. The lower the number, the better it sells. You should always do your own research. The best seller ranking is the best way to predetermine what items will have a better selling market.

Look at the competition. Look at who else is in your category. Do not chose products to sell that have larger name brands in the same category that you would be selling. You will be throwing yourself into instant, and tough, competition. People that shop for name brand, know it and will not want a newer version necessarily. If you have a good best seller ranking and little competition from big guys then that is a good sign.

You will want to scope out your competition. Look at the compitition's product revies. If they have less than fifty reviews that is also a good sign that it won't be too far away from achieving the same or surpassing them with a great marketing strategy.

What the reviews say is also important to deciding on your product. Look now at the reviews for the top three products like yours. You will want to look for the quality of the competition's products, consumer rankings, stars, and most importantly, any comments on the page (and how many). Look also at the number of products sold. Shoppers make quick but smart decisions based upon seeing these things so you should know what they are.

This is also where your own listing with great copy and great photographs will help. In tandem with consumer reviews, this information drives consumer purchases sometimes over price.

Consider your item as a gifts. Would it make a good one? These are some of the main reasons people shop online. Consumer goods and commodities are the next biggest. Gifts, Packaging, and shipping in Amazon boxes make gifts stand out to buyers who trust Amazon. Bundling puts products together that are complimentary. Always lookout for ways to increase the value of your item, and sales by bundling it with other products. Seasonal gifts may be less profitable year-round, although they are still a good niche.

If your product is an item that is not easily found elsewhere that is a good sign. See all of the other criteria in this chapter however as well. Specialty items and one of a kind products not found easily are a great lure for shoppers. Consider a specialized item. You will stand out with your unique feature or function.

Position your products to be better and different to stand out from the crowd. Make sure you point out the unique features in the listing in Amazon or on any multichannel programs for your FBA business.

Some products also succeed well if they were with other products or if they would be consumed often or used repeatedly by the consumer. Auto shipping is another feature than can complement this.

If you create the Private Label you can also create or buy an offshoot with a like product or a line to build you asset.

You want to look at your product as listed on Amazon, and review the key words.

Now, determine if the top three key words for your item have over 100,000 searches? A website such as at www.merchantwords.com as this information. High searches mean a higher demand.

Search also for the major 2-3 keywords for your product. Look as to if the other sellers have videos for their products. If so, that mean competition. You can also create one yourself that pulls up with great SEO on Google.

The third technique is to assess if there are also multiple keywords you can use for your items. Use more key words for a greater chance for a hit on a search and also a bestseller ranking or BSR.

Google has a great "keyword planner" tool also that will help you once you hone in on your category or products.

Instant and sustainable best sellers in most cases are impossible in the beginning when you first start to build your private label brands. The BSR should help shape your decisions. Again, look at Amazon's list of Best Sellers. Also look at the main category lists on eBay. Categories and sub-categories (thus some of your key words) are listed. Use this information along with cost, weight, durability, function, and so forth to shape your decision on a product. Individual quantities or units of each item as well as pricing and shipping information will be listed on each sourcing website if it is a large company.

As for where to find certain categories of goods, you will want to look at different sites. In general, it is most electronics and technology, clothes, and foods are not as popular on Amazon and eBay.

Alibaba is another website (www.alibaba.com) which focuses on a wide Asian and an international market. You will find items such as some health and beauty products, tools for the home, machinery parts, and accessories for dress.

Best seller lists may change, but in general items such as alarms and flashlights are small, light, and also cheap items, as are speakers and cameras for cell phones. Also, many people find useful anywhere in the world. Global Sources (found at www.globalsources.com) is another underutilized and lesser known place to source items. It is very much like Alibaba.

At sites like Global Sources you can source items from many different categories. They too have best seller lists. They even have live suppliers at large international trade shows.

Toys and gifts are generally well rated in almost platforms and sources.

Blogs, newsletters, websites, and list serves that might write about new and small simple gadgets contain valuable source information. You should sign up for these. A variety of blogs and websites for very specific purposes or for certain items (in areas like cooking or camping) may be good sources as well. Kickstarter.com and other crowdsource sites are also good resources. You can find very unique and new products here.

In just moving out and about, you may read or see new attractive tools or useful products. Trade shows in general are also good to visit. Recall that we want to buy in bulk straight from the supplier and make it an Amazon Private Label that we can sell as FBA across platforms.

Be creative ways in looking for products. The U.S. and China are the most popular for private label sellers. You will want to make sure that the product you want can be produced is available in bulk and that it can be and shipped to you first of all. You also want reputable suppliers. Alibaba calls these Gold Suppliers. Additionally, if there are vendors and more than one of these vendors supplies your product that is a good sign that you will have stock. You will want something like 500 units or so eventually to start a Private Label on Amazon. You also will have options for pricing most likely.

Chapter 6
How to make money

Whether you are on amazon or using any other platforms that contribute to the FBS, the original research that you do will help provide information as to if you should begin by buying certain items. When you set up your Amazon and multi-channel pages you have two options. You could list a small amount of really good products, or you could list large inventory. You do not know which the best way is until you get out there and try. Listen to examples from real life experiences as told by others who have successful Amazon businesses through the mentoring, forums, and videos as mentioned earlier.

You should look at the competition, which would include what they are selling and how many other resellers you determine are out there. You will also want to look at the model, year, size, availability, color, edition, price range, and condition, in addition to variables described earlier).

You may see that some products are in demand and yet that they are also available everywhere. In some cases, competition is good bur in others, an overkill of the same product is not desirable.

It is also a good idea to look at your competition and their shipping type and return policies are. These factors are beneficial and that just may give you an edge when you are ready to list and to sell as people love free and low-cost shipping

To do all of this initial legwork, you need simple tools: an obvious internet connection, smartphone or pad, some recommended Apps or other that you find, and/or a website to do some of the research mentioned prior. You can also talk to other retailers, and those who may be your sources for some advice on what the best sellers are or are not, and any product information or background that may help you.

Chapter 7
Increasing Sales with Marketing

Pay-per-click or PPC strategies are misunderstood, underutilized, and if done well, will lead you to increase sales. Once you have your items have sourced, stocked, and listed you want to market them for sales. Pay-Per-Click advertising, better known as simply PPC, works by converting your advertising into sales.

This is the way it works in general:

When shopping, and typing in key words for products, Amazon will pull up pictures and descriptions of both paid search results and organic searches. The organic search results appear to a shopper under the paid ads. They pop up because of search words and key words that you will set when listing as well as use in your Pay-per-click. On the top and/or right side are the paid-ads. Few people notice the difference. You should understand the difference in terms of your marketing.

By using pay-per-click, you target market your product better. By using a Pay-per-click campaign you are using a focused approach to identifying your customers and honing in on what they are looking for (which is your product!). You only pay for the ads as shoppers click on and open them. Data is also gathered from your own campaign and available to you for study and use.

You will set the:

- time frame

- key words

- budget

- as well as a few other variables

"Viewers" to the site should be converted to buyers. You do this by providing ads to send people to your products. Again, with pay-per-click you pay when shoppers click on the ads and show interest in the items. These campaigns can be quite cost-effective. The other great feature about the Pay-per-click campaigns is that they can be modified along the way. Your data will drive these marketing decisions as well. It is like having billboards and magazine ads but that you can go into the ads change often! You will need to know how to work with your key words, use reviews, and look at the ad groups.

There are two main part of the design of your Pay-Per-Click campaign, Part of this advertising strategy hinges upon setting up your ad campaign using Pay-Per-Click and the other part of the campaign involves the landing page where your products are showcased. Sales depend on the key words that bring people to your product pages on Amazon traffic and thus the sales. Some of the strategies for this are simple and some are much more advanced ones. You will learn about one approach that is good for any beginner.

The campaign launch is the first part to be developed. To bring in recurring streams of income you will be using Amazon for your selling. The pricing strategies also factor into the campaign development. Decide how much money you would like to spend in your Pay-per-click campaign for a week at a time. You

Consumer reviews are important but you need to earn them however. You will need to prove your worth. Your reiew pages and product pages will be your landing pages. You will see the product reviews for certain products when doing research for a particular product to source. To get great reviews, you begin with research. You will need first to make yourself stand out and encourage people to buy and use your product.

You should do product reviews from any one selling the same items as you, looking for name brands and other factors. For this strategy, you should make note of:

- What do their reports say?
- At what price is the product being sold?
- How many of the customer reviews does the product have?
- What key words they are using?

You may also see any PPC ads they may have placed. Look to see what types of information that you will need to gather your own product reviews for what products you purchased and own. You also want to look at this for other products that are already in the Amazon marketplace.

Study your competitor's pricing alongside looking at the reviews. You could take the strategy of lowering your product price to a bit less than that of your competitors, although not too much lower. You really want to present your product in a light so that you encourage reviewers to purchase and then comment honestly and positively on your goods.

Extras like coupon codes will help to send potential buyers to your products for some pre-determined period of time. In a way this is very much like persons who engage in consumer reviews and elect to receive items by snail mail. They will test out and then to write a consumer review in some format for the company.

There are also review service companies that you could purchase. You can also create your review services to do this. Per Amazon's guidelines (which you should also study), you will need to have your products legitimately reviewed as. Your consumers will have to make purchases that can be officially verified as legitimate by Amazon.

You could also get creative and offer incentives to get more customers to buy your new product and to provide you with an honest, and hopefully a positive, review. Read about Amazon's disclaimers that you will need to list somewhere on your site. When you look at other Amazon page reviews, you will see such disclaimers that you can use.

You will want and need some reviews to really establish yourself. The way that Amazon works is to attract people to the site, provide quick consumer information and provide quick and easy access to a product.

Amazon has review standards that you must follow. There are also target numbers that you can gather. To stay ahead of your competition, you need to monitor their sites as well as yours. Given that you probably have one product it should not be too difficult. Again, be careful of going up against name brands. It is very difficult to get sales and to grow a successful business in their shadow.

Your product eventually will turn up in search engines such as Google. That will come later. You will be progressing in a list of other sellers as you do well. Interestingly yet you may not show up on the top of the pages where your product is in line with other items. None of this yet concerns what we know about the best-seller rankings. With Pay-per-click advertising you will probably move up little by little if you do well in sales. You will drive traffic and move up the search rankings this way. You will be investing ad money.

You may also be lowering your product's original pricing for a period of time that is able to drive traffic to your landing page. As you collect advertising information from your new pay-per-click campaign, you will use that data to tweak how you sell products, get reviews and feed into that sales cycle. You will learn from this what was effective or not effective for the pay-per-click campaign.

The Pay-per-click campaign turns your ad clicks converted into actual sales. You want to design it so that anyone's mouse clicks on your personal ad will turn into money. It is that simple. Pay-per-click advertising also requires a different way of thinking. Other advertising works differently from the pay-per-click ad model on Amazon. Be open minded and we will guide you how to shape the campaign and read your data to improve it. As you see, listing products as FBA on Amazon or other platforms/channels is not just a matter of slapping some products on the page and selling them. It is a lot more involved.

Your business plan generally will outline what your costs versus your profits are. You also need to include an advertising budget. This section will help you to see what pieces of information you will need to plug in this specific budgetary item. You can always add or decrease funding on your own pay-per-click campaign as you go. You can also set a maximum cap for the ad campaign so that you won't go over the budget that you have set. If it is profitable, you should always add more money to the campaigns, and changing up what needs to be changed.

Data will show you the amount you are budgeting and what you have spent regarding the pay-per-click campaigns. In just a few weeks you should have enough data to look at trends.

Campaign costs are an important part of your set budget. As you research competitors and tweak your own campaigns, you will also start to look more closely at your product pricing. Do you need to increase or decrease the pricing? It is recommended to do so. By keeping pricing low for the item, you are encouraging people to try it and this should get you the reviews to establish your product and your brand. If you are doing well by that period of time and you are gaining sufficient reviews, you may think about staying a bit lower in your price. But you should work toward raising the price little by little.

Your profit margin will take into consideration specifically buying costs, shipping, and fees that we covered earlier, marketing and everything else mentioned thus far. Each site also has its fees so you are looking at multiple levels. At first you may have to keep things on the low side and sacrifice a bit of profit so that you can think longer-term and gather the following, the reviews, and the traffic that you need to start your product launch.

You must get good about doing regular key it is necessary although it does require time and focus. You will look at your data to see what drove people to your product through your ads. By that, it is meant, you will look to see what key words were helping to do this.

To effectively use the key words, put them:

- Directly in your title

- Bullet points about the product as far up as possible

- The item's listed description

If they work, use them to your advantage to draw traffic to your site to increase your ranking. Google's Keyword Planner is free if you set up a Google AdWords account (which is also free to use). It will help provide many key words that best fit your product from its database, and will provide other useful information. The search volume for each word is another good indicator. It is capable of ranking key words for your ads. You can add or change these new key words as you tweak your campaign.

You will use all of your data to shape your campaign, ads, and keywords, which is something else that is different than traditional advertising for products you have put on the market. The words that you create for your products not only shape the category where it may fall in Amazon, but they also drive traffic behind the scenes. You can also use them conversely not to draw words to you if you find that they deter people from purchasing your products. By adding these "negative keywords" and phrases to your campaign, your ads will not use them therefore won't draw them to your product.

If you get impressions of your ads but the impressions are not converting into buys then something is stopping this process from happening. The number of times that the PPC ads appear are the impressions. There are a few levels at which one can troubleshoot. You should look closer at some of the common areas that people lack in ad "optimization" to get the attention of the Amazon search engines.

If you recall, earlier we spoke of the importance of these following elements across Amazon and other channels that you intend to use Amazon FBA. It could be the fault of the photographs or images. They could be of a poor resolution, quality or color. The title may or may not have enough keywords. Descriptions should also be detailed, and use keywords as well. You don't want to pepper keywords like crazy, as this could create problems. Having too many stop words (fillers such as and, the, to, etc.) can also slow down search engines according to experts.

If there is an issue in the way your product displays in the search findings, it requires a bit more work. You will need to choose your keywords carefully and make them relevant to your product, or your product may be "lost" in the sea of Amazon pages. In essence, you could be buried in some other area if there are terms in your keywords that distract from what your product is. The keywords may be all right, but they may land you somewhere else. Keep your keywords relevant.

You should use popular as well as less commonly used keywords. You can also use three or more words together, called long-tail searches. These latter search words tend to drive the most traffic interestingly. If you find that the negative or less searched keywords have not led to sales, then shed them quickly, as they are just sitting around and may be costing you money. Remember that you are paying for each click in hopes in turns to purchase. Some people may choose to drop the words or phrases immediately, but another thought on this is to salvage search terms and use them in combination with other search words or terms. Another option is not to use them at all and bring them back as a test. A look at your advertising reports will help you make decisions such as on these issues. You also should play with word arrangements, using your data to the best of your ability.

Research your own keywords as well those for your competitors. Go to all of the sites mentioned in sourcing. Use these and your actual data to drive your ad words. Also, if you see your product's competitors using PPC ads for a while, it shows you that there is a market (either that or they are wasting money and do not know what they are doing!). You can test out this theory by looking at their product ranking and reviews, however.

Ad groups work in a similar way as how traditional advertising may run various campaigns to attract different consumers to the same product. You will improve the rates of your click-through as well as your rankings by splitting up your ads into different branches of your campaign. You may have to use different messaging to reach different markets.

You can create different ad groups and create cost-effective and scalable pay-per-click campaigns. By creating different ad groups, you are using keywords to shape a few mini-campaigns. By doing creating these various types of campaigns with their differing keywords that drive them to the same product you can take charge or your budget and see what is running well and what is running poorly.

From this information on your spreadsheet, you can see real numbers. You have your hard data. With a few calculations you can determine a few things just to start:

- What the profit margin was
- What the PPC cost was to advertise that product
- What search terms customers used to locate your product

For future ad word campaigns, you can incorporate the customer's search terms into your keywords. For your product information and searchable words within Amazon, you can include some of those new found words. If you cannot realistically fit the search terms into the name or title of your product, then perhaps you can locate a new place for them in the description area.

Chapter 8
Questions and Concerns

The Amazon FBA is not as cut and dry as it may seem. It creates some interesting concerns may arise about sourcing products. Some stores and some brands may not want their products bought and resold. This can happen for a variety of reasons. This is especially true for most of the larger name brands.

Some stores or other sources may limit amounts of products that can be sold, as or they may completely say no to the resale. Target is one company who is well known to enforce this internal policy

Reselling products through Amazon may threaten some businesses in their perception. This is not based in truth however. The perception is that you are being competitive with them. It is hard for many to see that the sales were made by the company at the start of the process. They were never lost anything with the product sale. From a business standpoint, they sold the product as they should have. In the cases where you may have sourced through a warehouse where the products would collect dust or possibly be destroyed, it costs them nothing less. Again, someone paid for their products.

Additionally, it adds to the market value of their product if it is still circulating on the market, which sometimes spreads internationally. It is also the way of more future business to come. It increases brand recognition and also may even create the desire by masses of consumers for the brand to continue their product that is being sold, to create new products, and even to revive older and favorite products.

Some stores and brands dislike the idea of a middle-man from a business perspective. Some try to cut the resellers out by forcing FBA to work with them solely and exclusively in order for Amazon to sell their product at all. It essentially sounds like retail extortion. This does not happen too often but it does happen with some.

The middle-man model also may give the perception that it cheapens their product. Some brands also may pressure platforms, such as Amazon to force retail sellers list that brand's particular item, to use certain labels to differentiate their brand with a resale that did not originate from them.

They also invest a lot of time, person power and money into advertising, marketing and tracking market values and price shifts themselves. Theoretically, the little retail Arbitrageurs is circumventing all of that, and sometimes with incredible success! A big store chain or brand company probably does not appreciate that fact. One might go so far as to also say that perhaps brands and stores should thank the retail Arbitrageurs for helping with these functions that would cost them much money to keep their products circulating and popular with buyers.

This is another area for consideration when starting an online business on Amazon you must check the laws of your particular state especially where business start-ups are concerned, as well as regarding taxes.

Most states will also require you to first establish yourself legally as a legitimate business entity. This is usually done through a consumer protection or commerce department but may vary from state to state. You will have to submit documentation and get written approval as well as an identification number. In some states, depending on the system as well as the type of business entity, you will get a state I.D. along with a federal I.D. You may be able to apply for tax-exemption as well.

The tax-exemption will serve a few purposes. You will not have to pay taxes twice. You already will have taxes through your platform, and then there would be retail taxes, and perhaps taxes on wholesale, warehouse and other source purchases that are conducted according to your own state laws.

Additionally, you would be hit with paying taxes on income at the end of the calendar year. In getting a status tax-exemption and using it for retailers and other source purchases, you are saving about one half of your potential taxes (which technically is not okay given that it is compounding and layering taxes, which is called pyramiding).

EBay and Amazon have integrated programs where you can handle all of your tax information from sales through their retailer/resale platforms. Otherwise, when you make sales online, you will have to worry about collecting and reporting and filing for different local and state taxes.

There are also apps and software programs such as Tax Jar to help you do this if you work with online sales. Again, the mantra is "do your research" and be smart about this very important and much overlooked aspect of your business.

If you purchase source products online, some retailers will accept a special exemption certificate which may list the type of goods that you are purchasing, and sometimes requires notation of the retail store, along with documentation of your tax identification number. You may have to call the headquarters and then fax these into a customer service department that handles tax-exemption.

Some stores will accept a certificate and form on the spot. It may take a manager or customer service representative to process it, just as a warning. This doesn't mean that you did something wrong, by the way. Store clerks may just not know what to do with it. Some stores won't allow a reseller to use a tax-exemption. A few of these are the ones who have banned retail Arbitrageurs entirely. More on this will come later.

Given that you are a home-based business you may be able to claim exemptions and get refunds for things related to your business such as travel, rent, telecommunications, supplies, etc. You should also check with a tax advisor or accountant.

Amazon also offers tools that take much of the out of the front end of collecting and calculating tax information that can be used for reporting to the federal IRS.

You will also need to verify with your state as well as determine what the online platforms need in order to resell merchandise. In some cases you will actually need an official license. You will need to also check with your state on this issue.

You will need to make sure you have all of the proper tax and reseller certificates, and that you are using them for their intended purpose and according to regulations. If not, you could may face serious consequences with the federal IRS and your state as well. You may also face losing a business license. Additionally, the platforms can, at any time, use their discretion to free or close down an online resale store.

Conclusion

Thank you again for purchasing this book, *Amazon FBA: A Scientific Breakdown of How to Build Your Own Profitable Amazon FBA Business*!

I hope this book was able to help you to understand what Amazon FBA is and how it works. This should be extremely useful if you are considering starting your own business.

The next step is to research your market and to come up with a clear business plan. Next you will need to set up your own platform accounts, plan on how to source items and do research before you list anything. If you follow the information and advice given to you in this book you will be on the path to success in Amazon FBA.

Finally, if you enjoyed this book, please take the time to share your thoughts and post a review on Amazon. It'd be greatly appreciated!

Thank you and good luck!

www.ingramcontent.com/pod-product-compliance
Lightning Source LLC
Chambersburg PA
CBHW070413190526
45169CB00003B/1240